A Beautiful Place to Die

A Beautiful Place to Die

Copyright©2022 Kimberley Atkinson

All rights reserved. No part of this work covered by the copyrights herein may be reproduced or used in any form or by any means—graphic, electronic, or mechanical—without the prior written permission of the publisher

ISBN# 978-1-988001-63-0

1. God 2. Christianity 3. Religion 4. Missions

Published in the United States of America

Printed in the United States of America

www.aheliapublishing@outlook.com

Dedication ...

To my favorite person on Earth, the woman who became my instant best friend half a world a way, in the desert of Kenya.

Eunice Njeri, I dedicate this book to you because I love you and this book exists only because you've encouraged me to write this story ever since we met.

Published & Printed in
Helena, Montana

A Beautiful Place to Die

Written by:
Kimberley Atkinson

Chapter 1

Now what? Who am I, really? What is expected of me? What should I do with my life? Do I matter? Please don't be silent, God. I need you.

It was a cold start to the new year as I sat in a chair I was declaring as my favorite. I gathered a small table to sit beside it, as well as a cup of tea, my Bible, and an empty journal. I was determined that even though I had boxes to unpack after the move, I would start my day on a more godly note and begin journaling. I had a small stack of mostly empty journals I had received as gifts over the years—none had more than a few pages of thoughts in them. I'd start, but the urge would pass quickly each time, and reality finally set in that I was not one of those journaling people. But as I sipped my tea this day, I determined in my heart that *this* journal would be different. How does one journal, exactly? Should I be writing my daily events, my daily thoughts, or going deeper with existential questions? My life was chaotic; we had just moved to a small town, my kids were now in a different school, I wasn't working yet … and there was the God element. Was I trying to be a better mom? Was I trying to be a better wife? Was I trying to know God deeper? What was my purpose? As I pondered such things this day, I sat in silence. I tried to quiet my erratic thoughts—make some ordered sense of them. I decided instead of me telling the journal what it was going to be about or trying to organize my thoughts into priorities, I would be open to what God was saying for me.

"I'm going to give you the desires of your heart." It was as though it had been said aloud in the room. My heart blossomed. I didn't realize how parched my soul was until it was given the living water of hope. I repeated it out loud to hear it on my own lips. "I am going to give you the desires of your heart." It felt right in my spirit. I chose in that moment to believe those words were truly God's wish for me. My mother's voice entered my mind right then, as she liked to say, "God said it, I believe it, that settles it." That did settle it. I knew He had spoken, just as confidently as I knew my own name. His words were becoming a part of my existence. His Word was shaping my destiny. His words … *If only I knew what His words meant* … I laughed to myself as I realized I had no idea what to do with His words. But it was a start, so I wrote it down.

Soon the sounds of my family waking up filled the hallways and bathroom and kitchen. I'd try to sit down earlier tomorrow, but right now I was pulled back into the practicum of life. I made lunches and found lost socks, all with a promise ringing over and over in my mind about a desire that would be fulfilled. I re-woke a couple of the kids, still wondering what desire would be met by God. I prepared breakfast, but I couldn't stop thinking of the chair that sat in the next room with my new journal, and the one sentence I had written down. The chair was beckoning me to return.

Over the next month, I tried valiantly but disastrously to return to the chair on a regularly timed schedule. I wanted to repeat what had happened. I wanted to gain more insight. I wanted more than one sentence in my journal. I wanted to understand.

I thought, "How does one go about choosing a top desire?" If God said He would fulfill the desire of my heart, I wanted it to be a really well-chosen desire. I felt like I had the ultimate *Get One Free Ticket,* and I didn't want to waste it on anything frivolous. I began formulating options that only God could handle, like a proverbial top ten list of desires, thinking I would be happy if He chose any one of them.

"You didn't hear Me correctly ... I'm going to *give you* the desire of your heart. I'm going to place a desire in your heart, and then I'm going to make you desire it so greatly that you are going to beg Me to grant it to you." Oh God, please no. My *Get One Free Ticket* just went up in smoke. My top ten list dissipated into thin air. I didn't even want to write His answer into my journal. I didn't want to make it real. I didn't want it etched into any existence that I would have to read over and over again. My heart restricted. I knew what He was going to choose ... it was my greatest fear ...

My mind immediately reeled back in time to before I was a

Christian. My mom and dad were recent converts to Christianity in my remembered memory. I wasn't opposed to the decision personally, but I was a young teenager and was stalling. My mom had begun hosting visiting missionaries from their church. I remembered sitting around the dining room table and hearing horrifying stories of what it was like to be a missionary for God. There was always lack, always calamity, always intense cultural clashes. And then those missionaries would talk and laugh and get so excited as they would share how it would take the God of the Universe to rescue them from the situation. Next visiting missionary, same terrifying stories, same result. I began to wonder if this was to be their last meal at my table. What if the God of the Universe was too busy one day to keep taking care of them? What if He looked away at the wrong moment and they weren't rescued? What if He chose not to help? Who would ever willingly sign up to be a missionary in Africa?

Oh, God, please no … we had an agreement. At least, I believed we had one. I remembered that moment just as clearly. I meant it when I had said it. I had told God that I would become a Christ follower and would serve Him all my life, but in return, He would agree not to send me to Africa. We had made a covenant. Hadn't we? I hadn't stopped living for Him, so why would He do this to me?

My journal now had two sentences and my heart did not feel as fulfilled as I had imagined it would be upon the second entry. I put the journal away. Why had I even started? I wanted to shelve this potential future as well, but as much as I tried to erase it from my mind, it only grew in intensity. I knew He was going to fulfill this word. I knew He was faithful to complete what He had started in me. I had nowhere to run; no place to hide. I could mentally picture a tight rosebud suddenly burst and begin to unfold. I tried to cry out to Him about my fears, but all I could picture was the next petal popping out of its tight pose. I tried to use my family and small children as an excuse to stay put in our new town—which was nowhere near Africa. The rose petals opened wider. I tried to tell the Lord I had no finances to go to Africa. The exterior petals loosened. The more arguments I could think to use in this futile argument just worked against me. The rose was in full bloom now. I couldn't fold it back inside of itself now even if I had wanted to. Only the God of the Universe could do that, and He didn't desire to do so. He had a different desire to fulfill.

The months passed quickly and painfully. The desire grew and couldn't be replaced. It was like someone was stuffing gunpowder into a keg, and if they kept going it would blow up. I was about to blow. I wanted it, I desired it, every ounce of my being longed to go to Africa. But where? How? I needed to figure out a plan on how to relieve the pressure in the midst of, and despite my fears. I wanted to be an overcomer, but it was hard to imagine being on another continent—one that I had feared for so long.

Spring had come and with it many blooming flowers and warm skies. My thoughts went to Africa. What would the flowers there look like? What would a warm day feel like? What would the air smell like without pine trees? I couldn't stop the swell of desire and emotion to be in a place I'd never gone before. Surely it was irrational to still be scared by something I wanted so badly, wasn't it? How could I feel both?

I hadn't brought out that journal again. I just couldn't imagine my life if God were to add anything more right now, but I remember when the telephone rang. It was an American friend with an odd request. He had been praying and had felt led of God to ask if I wanted to join him and some of his friends on a trip to Africa. I quickly agreed. I didn't care where specifically, in fact, I didn't really want to know many details. I just knew my powder keg was overstuffed. He shared a few of the most important details, like on what day we would meet in Amsterdam, and assured me he would take care of the arrangements. It all sounded great to me, as I just couldn't take in a full discussion with endless details. He ended the call by making sure I understood there was a short deadline to pay for the tickets, and to bring $200 US cash along for the final flight. Again, I quickly agreed, said goodbye and hung up.

I'm not sure if this left me with a resolution to my problem or actually managed to create a bigger problem for me. Now I had to go. But I wanted to go. But I was still scared. But I had promised I'd be there. But I had no money. But God was giving me an unquenchable desire. But, but, but …

I now had a date and a destination and a desire but was fighting dread in my mind. I grew more conflicted as the date drew near. On one hand, I shared with my parents what was happening and they were praising God. On the other hand, I wasn't really telling friends around me, so we didn't have to talk about it. I started making buns and cinnamon buns to sell. It was a small effort and a small reward, but I genuinely thought that if the day came to fly out and I still didn't have the funds, God would let me off the hook. I would say I had tried but came up short. Surely the Lord didn't want me to go into debt doing this, did He?

The week of flying out finally arrived and I was nowhere near having the full ticket value let alone any excess for while I was there. I was quite proud of my escape route plan and believed it had succeeded for a moment—only a moment—until God showed up in power and might.

I had been helping a friend one evening with a computer problem and when I returned home, I discovered some cash in my jacket pocket. I quickly called her back to reprimand her for paying for my aide only to discover she hadn't given me the money. I laughed at myself for getting so nervous around money and let it go. A couple of my kids overheard the conversation and thought it so funny that I had forgotten about some cash in my jacket that they decided to check the other pockets in case I had forgotten more; and they found more. There was no way I had left even more cash, because I had already checked all of my pockets. I thought my kids were playing a prank on me. I knew there shouldn't be any more cash, but there they were, holding it out to me. I grabbed my jacket once more and checked all the pockets only to find even more bills. Surely there was no earthly way I had misplaced all those bills … no earthly way at all. But there was a heavenly way.

I thought, "Oh no … not again." God was removing my contingency plan. He was making a way. I fell to my knees in repentance and thanked God for every bill coming out of that jacket. Then, I finally did what I should have done months earlier and called over my friends and the pastor and told them about this desire to go to Africa, about my fears, about the phone call, and about the flights coming up that week. Then I told them about the jacket—and the money. We took turns that evening reaching into the pockets of that coat and pulling out the blessings He was miraculously placing there. There was more than enough for the plane tickets and supplies. The only thing missing was the American money I was supposed to have on me for the fifth plane into the interior of Mozambique. I noticed it was missing from the jacket, so I had a slight revision to my contingency escape plan. I decided not to mention it and to take just enough flights to land in Africa, but then not continue inland with my friends but instead return home. Surely that would be enough to relieve the pressure of the powder keg within me while also honoring this new desire to go to Africa. God would accept this new plan, right?

I saw the kids through to the end of school, and they were as ready for their summer holidays as I was for Africa. What would the summer hold for all of us? Would we each have stories to share as it ended? Hopefully, if I had a story, it wouldn't be one of those terrifying dinner table stories.

Chapter 2

Now what? Who am I, really? What is expected of me? What should I do with my life? Do I matter? Please don't be silent, God. I need you.

Here I sit, on the plane, en-route to Africa. I know we haven't left the tarmac yet, but I can hardly believe the moment is here. Only because of miraculous provision could I afford this, so I am feeling most humble. Only because He put a desire in my heart, am I wanting to be here. I have a smile on my lips and anticipation in my heart. The powder keg is full, but it's about to be relieved. As the people are making their way down the aisle to their seats, I am watching to see who my seat-mate might be. An elderly lady signals that the window seat beside me is hers, and I'm happy to jump up and make way for her. As we settle back in, we say hello to each other and she asks me the most natural question in the world for people about to fly together, "Where are you headed?" I pause. Where exactly am I headed? I know it's in Africa, but I wasn't wanting to hear too many details, so I'm not exactly sure. I'm not even sure what the plan is once we get there, but maybe that doesn't matter because I still have my contingency escape plan. This was all probably more information than this sweet old lady wanted to hear on such a mundane question, so I just mutter, "Mozambique," hoping she doesn't want more information.

Apparently, *Mozambique* is a trigger word because it changed the very persona of this sweet old lady into a fierce, angry woman with a furrowed brow, flared nostrils and pursed lips, who emphatically snarled, "I do not believe in God and you cannot pray for me."

"Okay," was all I could think to respond. I was stunned. What did she know that I didn't know? Why was she so angry at just the sound of this African country? Oh Lord, what have I done? Oh Lord, what have *You* done?

She shifted her body to face more toward the window and abandoned our contact. My smile dimmed, and the flame of anticipation so bright in my heart only minutes before started to flicker out. My fears were starting to rise and so was my heart rate. The only thing that broke me out of myself was when all the oxygen masks fell from the overhead compartments which contained them, and the captain's voice came over the cabin intercom: "Attention all passengers. Please follow the directions of your flight attendants. Please leave all personal belongings and move to the emergency exits as quickly as possible as there is a fire onboard."

There was no more time to think about my seat-mate or my fate in Africa. It was time to ensure I wasn't sticking around to be engulfed in flames. As the smoke started to fill the cabin, there was a lot of pushing from behind me, encouraging those before me to slide down the inflatable emergency slide more quickly. I had never exited the side of a plane before, and I imagined no one else had either. Fire trucks were racing across the tarmac and grass. As we landed at the bottom of the slide, we were quickly herded into a long shuttle bus that had met us. There was panic and fear and tears from my fellow passengers. We were all safe, but we were rattled. I had thought, "Lord, can I go home now? I came, I tried, but it wasn't meant to be. Maybe we could try this another time?" The Lord was silent. I guessed that wasn't a *yes*, so I stayed inside the shuttle bus along with everyone else, wondering what the airline was going to do with us. It wasn't long before they announced they had found us another plane and we were all going to be reloading shortly—which was exactly what we did.

Round two of loading passengers was very different from round one. As we left the shuttle bus, we all were asked how we were feeling, and if we had any injuries. We then walked, mostly shrouded in silence, across the grass and up a staircase into the next plane. It was a strange feeling to find our seats again and look into the eyes of strangers we had only met for mere minutes, but who were now kindred strangers after experiencing a traumatic event together. Everyone had an unspoken bond—everyone except for me and my seat-mate. Apparently, this shared occurrence still wasn't enough for this sweet old lady to forgive me for my original "Mozambique" response, and she huffed and fumed to see I had resumed my position beside her once again. The second plane took off and everyone cheered. It helped break the somber mood. People still whispered to each other in hushed tones as we all held our collective breath that we would just make it safely to our destination in the States. When the captain announced we were preparing for descent, we all cheered again. Again, everyone except for this once, long ago, sweet old lady.

As we were approaching the city and the landing strip, my seat-mate finally spoke to me. "I still don't believe in God, and you still can't pray for me. But I do believe in evil, and I think that the last plane caught fire because of you." I was shocked again! How could she think that? I hadn't done anything to her or to the plane. Why was she so furious with me? She continued, "I'm trying to figure out how to combat that evil and this is all I can think to do." She reached down for her wallet, opened it up, and gave me all she had in it—exactly $200 American dollars. I was shocked again but this time for an entirely different reason. I tried to thank her, but she didn't even want me to talk to her. God, I'm so sorry. I knew I boarded that plane without the money I was told ahead of time to have. I knew I was creating excuses so I wouldn't have to commit fully to Africa. I was still letting my fear dictate my actions and thoughts instead of my faith and commitment to

Christ. Once again, I needed to repent. And I probably needed to ask forgiveness of all my fellow kindred strangers who had to endure a plane catching fire just so God could teach me this lesson. But I hear you now, Lord. I am Yours. You wanted me here and there was going to be no thwarting of that plan by any ill-devised schemes. It was time once and for all to let go of all my fear and embrace the desire of my heart.

Shortly after arrival in the United States, I boarded my connecting flight to Amsterdam, with a boisterous group who apparently had no awareness of how quickly flying could turn to terror. But I had the American dollars now firmly in my possession, with a fresh lesson in my heart, so I was determined to shake off the overshadowing of doom from the last plane and start looking forward to the continent to where my heart's desire was pulling me.

The city of Amsterdam was within sight; we were in descent now and I was looking forward to meeting up with my friend. But reunions were about to be put on hold. Suddenly, all the lights in the cabin went black and the oxygen masks dropped before our faces ... again. The sycophancy of noise began to swell and my heart dropped. I could see the airport. I could see the runway. We were so close ... I could see the fire trucks coming. Now I knew we were in trouble. Someone was yelling to *brace ourselves*; it might have been the flight attendant or it might have been the hundreds of voices repeating it. "Oh God, no," was also being repeated out loud as well as in my head. How could this be happening?

The plane hit the tarmac … hard. We remained in forward motion. The fire trucks closely escorted us. This was probably my biggest sense of comfort, so I fixed my eyes on them outside the window, and willed them to not fall behind. I was unaware of any smoke inside the cabin or flames outside the cabin, so it seemed we were just riding a brakeless tube. We rode it until the runway ran out. Then we rode it across grass, which was extremely bumpy and caused many people to erupt in frantic cries of woe. I did not sense a slowing down on the grass, but we learned the difference between a bumpy ride and an abrupt stop when we hit something big and hard at the end. Those not in crash positions with their heads down and gripping their legs were thrown the hardest. Praise God, I was so terrified I hadn't dared to move out of my position, so I wasn't injured when the crash finally happened.

Now for the second time in the same day, the side emergency doors were quickly opened, and the inflatable slide was ready for evacuation. Twice in the same day I made the unorthodox descent to the ground. Twice in the same day I was quickly evacuated to a waiting shuttle bus.

We were the lucky ones.

I stared out the window, watching some fellow passengers being strapped onto emergency boards and loaded into waiting ambulances. The shuttle bus was filled with people inside their own heads, frozen in disbelief, staring out the windows at the carnage which only moments earlier had been our plane. They were thanking whatever deity they prayed to that this hadn't happened over the ocean and that they were safe on solid ground. I prayed to my Lord, the God of Heaven, the Creator of all things who didn't look away at the moment I needed Him the most. I prayed to my personal Savior who had saved me into eternal life once back when I was 14, and now twice more today.

Inside the terminal, I met up with my friend and those traveling with him. As we shared our travel experiences thus far, I inadvertently filled my new travel cohorts with valid concerns about flying with me. I hadn't thought of that before. Was I the common denominator? I might have to own responsibility for the plane that caught fire, but was the plane crash due to me as well? I thought I had repented. I was trying to leave my fear behind. Was there something else I was supposed to have done? My heard swirled with thoughts and wonderings.

With much relief to both myself and my new group, we made it safely to Johannesburg for the night. I did it. I had officially walked on African soil. My senses were confused a bit though—it looked just like a modern city. I think all I had ever seen of Africa were commercials of crying orphans in dirt huts put forth by organizations looking for donations to feed the poor. I didn't see a single dirt hut or a single crying, shoeless child, but it all still felt foreign. My friend quickly organized a couple of cabs to take us to our hotel for our first overnight stay before we continued in the morning with our flights out of South Africa and on toward Mozambique.

Mozambique ... the trigger word for the sweet old lady on my first plane, the same sweet lady who had been enraged at a single word then had given me the 200 American dollars that were still safely tucked away in a zippered pocket. Mozambique ... the foreign destination that had captivated my heart without my ever setting foot in it. Mozambique ... where the powder keg in my spirit would truly be relieved. Mozambique ... where God would give me the desires of my heart.

We were ushered quickly and quietly into the hotel and warned not to come out and not to stand at the windows; and no matter what we witnessed, we were not to stop it or to intervene. The cab drivers told us they would be there in the morning for us, so I casually entered the hotel and didn't even take notice that right after our luggage was removed from the trunks, so were their automatic weapons as they stood guard over their charges and the hotel we slept in that first night.

Chapter 3

Now what? Who am I, really? What is expected of me? What should I do with my life? Do I matter? Please don't be silent, God. I need you.

I awoke early the next morning, partly due I'm sure, to jet lag, which I had never experienced before, and partly due to foreign sights and smells and sounds just outside of my window. My room was on the second floor of the hotel, so I couldn't resist the urge and therefore ignored last night's warning and stood at my window to take in all my eyes could see. I saw some green trees, but mostly concrete and a dust that seemed to settle on everything. Buildings were jammed together with thick concrete support walls but seemed to stand precariously unstable; maybe it was all the additional supporting sticks dug into the ground bracing those same walls at strange angles. The hoards of people who flooded all the available ground, whether around the base of the buildings or filling the curbs and onto the roads, was innumerable. I had never seen inside an ant colony before, but this is what it reminded me of—thousands of people moving their own directions, parting crowds of thousands more going their own way; whether that be to work or home I wasn't sure.

I watched with interest as a vehicle hesitantly approached the intersection beside the hotel. I watched in shock as it hit a disabled pedestrian then just kept driving. I watched in horror as a small mob overtook this same car stopped at the red light, and started beating it for the injury it had just caused. I watched in confusion as the driver handed money out his window to the defending mob. I watched in disbelief as the mob ceased their rant, allowed the car on its way, and then shared their gains with one another. I watched in understanding as they all took their original positions, even the disabled pedestrian, who suddenly appeared to be quite mobile. I watched with pity as the next vehicle approached and the performance was repeated. I removed myself from the window before I was noticed. The last thing I needed was for the next performance being geared toward this unsuspecting tourist.

    Had I come to impact these people? Or had God sent me to be impacted by this nation? What are You up to, Lord? Silence. I tried to stifle the fear that threatened to rise as we made our way back to the airport that morning. We were warned that we wouldn't stop if we hit anyone, and I knew why. We were warned not to allow anyone to help us with our bags. We were warned not to purchase any water outside of the airport. We were warned to never use the washrooms alone. We needed to stay in small groups at all times. Inside the terminal, we were warned not to make it appear as if we had never been here before but instead to discuss our supposed memories out loud and act as if we knew exactly where we were headed. It was an act, but I had a part to play. I dreaded that if my upcoming performance was not Oscar-worthy, I would be ferreted out and a riot would ensue—overpowering me much like that poor vehicle this morning. I didn't want to do or say anything wrong and receive an adverse reaction from the local crowd.

Lord, I have a feeling You love these people, but right now I fear them. Please help me to see them through Your heart of love. Please help me to quell the wave of fear and emotion threatening to shatter the performance mask I am wearing right now. Will there come a time when I can just be myself? Am I safe? It is so easy to judge a culture just by comparing it to our own. The fear of the unknown is always greater than the fear of the known.

With Johannesburg and South Africa behind us, we set flight once again toward our destination. Our landing place was quaint but with the same sense of unstable buildings and dust that clung to everything. There were less people about, but that could have been because we stayed inside the airport terminal. I had the feeling that the majority of the local population didn't do much flying. At long last came the final flight into the heart of this new nation. I pulled out my 200 American dollars, handed it to a local man gathering the funds and was given a piece of paper on which he had written my name and a future date and time. I was told to keep this paper safe because it was my return ticket. Without it I would not be able to re-board this flight, so I safeguarded it in the zippered pocket of my skirt. I knew we were transitioning to a more rural area, but I didn't expect the plane to feel so precarious. My troubles were already apparent on much larger, safer looking planes than this one, so sitting in my white plastic lawn chair bolted and tied down in single file against the walls of the cabin inside the plane was almost more than my fragile emotions could handle. God, please don't let me burn or crash or whatever could happen! As the pilot prepared for takeoff, I was inside my own head re-evaluating my life choices and praying my best prayer for supernatural and miraculous provision for a safe, and hopefully gentle, arrival at our final landing spot.

With my fears in my throat we took off. And although we soared quite peacefully, my spirit did not. It was time to get my heart right. I'm sorry, Lord. I think I was looking for something to justify my fears rather than looking to You to give me stability and peace. I was looking out the hotel window on this experience rather than knowing I was in Your arms. You had asked me to come. You had put the biggest desire of my life into my heart. You had me protected at every angle. And You loved this nation and these people. Lord, allow me to love them like You love them. Allow me to see them the way You see them. Allow me to represent You well.

With hardly a bump the pilot expertly landed his craft and we began to file out. From the top of the steps where the door opened all I could see was land. Gone were the propped up buildings. Gone were the crowds. This was raw. It was untouched. It was gorgeous. There was an occasional short type of scrub brush, and even more occasionally, a thin tree stood with them. Spires of dust clouds arose from the dirt, reminiscent of the fragile columns of a colosseum about to be created by a child. How strange to have everything look familiar yet so foreign in their configurations. The sun was high in the sky and took the temperature right up with it. With every breath my lungs warmed up with the African air and learned to filter out the fine dust that came with it. I remember putting Chapstick on my lips thinking I was going to prevent them from drying out. Instead, they became gritty.

We had landed beside the largest of the trees visible for miles, so I could see why it was a good landmark. The distance was also spotted with slightly round dirt igloos I could only assume were either homes or at least domes created for shade. Beside this tree was a makeshift stall you might see at a pop-up farmer's market—a stall without many wares to sell, but a worker nonetheless. It took me a moment to realize this too was a part of the "airport" and I affectionately branded it the "duty-free" shop in my mind. I wondered if this poor boy stood out here all alone every day hoping to sell what he had, or if there was an actual flight plan he somehow was made aware of and had set up for the tourists. Either way, many of my new group made their way to his stall to reward his smiles and waving with purchases.

We stood around his stall until we heard a vehicle coming from far off. We could only assume its passengers also knew where the "duty-free" shop and landmark tree were, and what had just been offloaded. Once the truck arrived there were a few introductions and welcome hugs for my friend. Then we, with our luggage in tow, were all encouraged to climb into the back of the truck and settle under the tarp stretched across the back. My mind made the assumption that this action was required to ensure we wouldn't get dirty as we raced across the desert, but the warning to not move or be loud implied a more ominous, practical reason. I didn't want to ask because I didn't want to know. It took me this last flight to get my heart as right as possible, and I was determined to just experience what God had for me. Fear did not need to ruin it.

I was moderately content under that tarp. I had chosen a

soft-sided backpack style case to bring with me, so I laid upon it and let the bouncing of the truck over the rough landscape become a part of the experience. I laughed to myself, thinking how my two sons would have liked this and treated it as a game, so I hung on as tightly as I could to my bucking bronco of a suitcase to make them proud.

I may have dozed, but it didn't seem an excessively long time before we slowed and I could hear other voices milling about the exterior of the truck. I hadn't thought about my placement getting in, but at that moment I was glad I wasn't near the sides of the truck box. Because of their foreign language, I couldn't tell if they were friend or foe, so I gripped my case and kept my body still and my jaws and eyes clamped shut.

Thank God they were friends. The tarp was pulled back and we were met with grins, handshakes, hugs, and a helping hand to disembark. I could now see that we were inside a compound as there were large wooden walls obstructing any view of the outside desert world I had seen already. Inside this compound were some concrete bunkhouse style buildings around the exterior and a large open-sided shelter you could see was a kitchen of some sort. There were worn paths in the dirt leading from doorway to doorway between the buildings where all shrubs were either pulled or worn down. There was one large tree also near the exterior wall in an unobstructed area where children played beneath. I don't know what that tree was originally, but it looked like God had ripped it out of the earth and put it back in with the roots to the sky. Touching it felt like what I imagined a leg of an elephant would feel like—a bit leathery and it would indent slightly if I pushed hard enough with my thumb.

I had made it. I was in Africa. And Africa was greeting me with enthusiasm. The children ran circles around me like I was the May pole. We were greeted by the organizers of the orphanage. An orphanage? I was playing with little orphans in Africa just like in the commercials I had seen, except these ones were full of joy in their lack. We were told we could set up our tents under the strange tree on the open ground. Tents? Was that one of those details I so conveniently didn't listen to? I didn't have a tent so the organizers directed me to one of the smaller buildings which held supplies. I was offered to go find one in there to set up.

The supply building didn't hold many useable supplies at all. There were bits and pieces of discarded items piled upon each other. It looked like these supplies were items discarded by outsiders but treasured by those inside these compound walls. My eye fell on a canvas bag that said *Personal Tent* so that is what I grabbed. I hauled it back to the open ground and began to set it up. At least all the pieces were there. It ended up being a small red dome about four feet by four feet. It was small but it was perfect. I loved it. I wasn't sure where the rest of the arriving party dispersed to, but I was the first to set up, so I chose a spot right below the root-looking tree.

My friend and most of his travel companions were in meetings with the orphanage organizers for the evening, so I spent my time running with the kids and setting up my new little living space. I couldn't stand upright in my tent, but it still seemed to really suit me. It was my first evening in the desert of Mozambique and one of my new teammates offered up his satellite phone so I could phone home and let my family know I had arrived safely, since they had probably been tracking the issues with the first two flights. I thought that was a really sweet idea, so I wandered the compound with the phone in the air in attempt to find a signal.

"Hello?" It was so good to hear a familiar voice. "I just wanted to let you all know I arrived safe and sound in case you were watching the news or tracking the flight information for my first two plane rides." Silence. I was told no one was paying attention as they were dealing with the death of my husbands' grandmother that had occurred since I had left. I quickly passed along my condolences and ended the call, since they all had greater grief to deal with than my crazy flight stories.

As I bunked down for the night I thought of a grandmother, who, though her family missed her greatly, was exactly where she wanted to be: in the arms of Jesus. This made me realize I was exactly where Jesus wanted me to be: also in His arms. We were both in a miraculous place that our hearts had longed for. I wouldn't make it home for the funeral but at least they all had each other.

Good night, family ... Good night, Lord.

Chapter 4

Now what? Who am I, really? What is expected of me? What should I do with my life? Do I matter? Please don't be silent, God. I need you.

Loud Muslim prayers filled the sunrise. I could hear them over the wall. I didn't know if we were right beside a mosque or if the sheer number of outside people chanting together created the symphony. Inside the compound there was a different type of commotion. I laid there, curled up on top of my blanket on the soft sand bottom and listened to both streams of noise and tried just to focus my mind on my own early morning prayers. Soon the commotion inside the compound took over and I realized people weren't just moving about my tent, brushing up against it, they were actually trying to shake it and get my attention. I unzipped the door and was met with children and other African adults eager for me to emerge and kneel and pray with them. I thought at first this was something I should have known about and was late for but soon realized there was no specific occasion, just people coming to pat me on the back, smile, and bow with hands clasped toward me. I was uncomfortable in my confusion.

I looked around for my friend thinking he could interpret what was happening for me, but he was nowhere to be found. What I did see was a huge bloom hanging from the root tree under which I had put my tent. Then it was explained to me that the big old root-looking tree only bloomed every 5 to 50 years, and no one could ever remember it blooming yet. If it didn't bloom, it didn't create the seeds which they so desperately needed. But there it was, a bloom the size of my head, hanging low and just about touching my tent. The people didn't want me out of the tent, they were just trying to get close enough to see the bloom. The adults and kids were celebrating its very existence and because it had bloomed last night while I slept under it, they thought I would like to join in on the celebration.

It was a new day on a new continent, and it had begun with celebration of a long-awaited promise. I had awoken that morning in the same space and time as a declaration from the Father of Creation to a people whom He loved. Emotionally, the moment was powerful. There were chants outside the walls to a God who could not hear or react. Inside the wall was the answer to a promise and prayers passed down through generations. The answer is that my God hears and can react. The answer is that God provides. The answer is that God has blessed this exact day and now this day felt alive with potential. The answer is that I felt very honored it bloomed above my head like a personal sign from God directly to me that He will take care of me too. I was ready for anything.

Or so I had thought. Not too much later, my friend arrived in our area of the compound to share the news that the orphanage organizers had to leave. The wife had fallen very ill in the night due to Malaria and the husband had taken her in search of medical treatment. There had been a pre-organized plan to take the Jesus film into the remote villages, at the acceptance of the chiefs, and show it to the local people. Wow, an untouched people group! I had only heard that as a colloquial term before now, but they were about to become real. And I was going to meet them.

The interim director requested that anyone who wanted to go should pack a tent along with a few belongings and get back into the truck box once again. Several people moved quickly, but before they could disperse too far, the warning of reality was levied. Outside the compound were Muslim: Jihad Muslim … it wasn't safe. If they asked us if we were Christian, we needed to be ready with our answer. If they discovered we were, they would be celebrated when they killed us. They could not guarantee anyone's safety. I paused. Several thoughts flooded my mind all at once: the flower, the fact that I didn't get hurt in my flights, and that the tribal chiefs knew we were coming. Surely we wouldn't get hurt by people we were actually invited to minister to, would we? I pushed aside my fear; I wouldn't let it keep me stuck in immobility. I pushed aside what I had seen from the hotel window; I wouldn't let it color my perception of these people. You had asked me to come, Lord, and I don't think You meant just to sit under a tree of promise. I packed up my little red dome, put my belongings into my backpack, then jumped up into the back of the truck. Large white envelopes were passed around. Everyone who had decided to come was told to put their money, identification, passports, and all other valuables like the return tickets in it, so they didn't get lost or damaged out in the bush for the next few days. I did as I was told. I handed over my valuables, took my seat, took some deep breaths, and allowed excitement to wash over me. If only my children could see me now! If they were proud of me for riding my bucking suitcase, they would be cheering to see me off on this adventure.

    For the next several hours, we bumped along our own rural route. People stared from the doorways of their own dirt dome houses, and children ran alongside us like pods of dolphins. We would stop and there would be conversations held in local native tongues which I imagined to be invitations to join the movie tonight. Only twice did we get out of the truck, but each time we were greeted with smiles and were told this village had just chosen their new pastor. He was going to ride with us now, and return to the orphanage with us as well, for pastoral training in a few days. I may not have understood the structure of how pastors were chosen, but maybe it was to choose a young man with the biggest grin because each young new pastor we picked up was more joyous and animated than the last. They would greet us with muscled hugs and hearty claps on our backs as if we were long lost friends. It was hard not to feel genuinely happy to see them as well as they boarded the truck bed.

As we made our first official stop where the movie would be shown that evening, the approval in the air was decidedly less welcoming than that which we had received from the newly chosen pastors en-route. People stood afar with crossed arms and suspicious eyes. No children were allowed to play near us. In fact, the only people close to us were completely covered in what appeared to be white chalk paint. They wore unusual headdresses and half stomped, half yelled in our direction to make it obvious they didn't want us there. Our interpreters informed us they were witch doctors trying to curse us and recommended we pray against the curses when we hear them shout. I'd never seen a witch doctor before, let alone prayed against their curses, but I definitely gave it my best effort. It was hard not to watch and give them a stage, but I was trying not to let them rattle me. Sticks and stones and all that. Maybe it was good I didn't know their language right then.

A crowd gathered as we rolled out the extension power to a generator, trying to put it as far from the movie watchers as possible. We set up the projector on the box it was stored in and directed the light at the makeshift movie screen. The screen had been fabricated with a large sheet stretched around poles coming out of the top holes in the long side of the truck bed. I think we were ready. The local pastors who had journeyed out with us started to clap and sing and dance in the dirt. Some people watching began to join in. Again, I didn't know the language, but it seemed to be a song they all knew, so I could only assume it had nothing to do with Christ yet. Maybe this was a way to get them engaged. It worked, as more and more gathered to sing and joined in.

The witch doctors who were front and center were soon moving off to the side, but I kept them in my periphery because it seemed a prudent thing to do. The whitest amongst our group, myself being one, couldn't master the rhythm of the stomping dance and didn't sing the words correctly, so all I garnered were the belly laughs of the children. It was enough to begin to break through the barriers of cultural unfamiliarity.

The singing and dancing seemed to last well past sunset, which is what we had needed in order to project the film. I remember looking into the unrecognizable pattern of stars in the night sky. It seemed like there were substantially more stars than I was used to, possibly even in the Milky Way, judging from the sheer amount. Again, the sky was not something I had considered would also appear unfamiliar in this land of unfamiliar.

Finally the chief spoke, and through our own interpreter we discovered what he was saying. He told the crowd that we were there to show a movie about God that he did not believe and that the only reason he had agreed for us to come was that he had heard of sick people becoming well in other villages. Then the chief declared there were going to be conditions for us to show the film. He was going to bring in his four sickest tribal members and expected them to become healed instantly and completely or we agreed to forfeit our lives. There wasn't much time to talk amongst ourselves. I was in denial that we were even in this precarious position. I'm a mother; I have kids at home; I can't die in Africa. We kept asking the interpreter to repeat what the chief had said in case he had either interpreted it incorrectly or we had heard him incorrectly. Over and over I heard the ultimatum. My anxiety rose and my faith disappeared. They brought in the sick and lined them up in front of us. The first was a woman who was paralyzed, and they had placed her and her mat down in front of us. Next, they brought in a blind man who we could tell immediately wasn't blind due to cataracts, but instead to the actual lack of eyeballs. We could see his infected, dirt-filled sockets. The third was a young boy on crutches who was missing a leg, which the interpreter informed us was because of land mines. And lastly, they helped an older man to the front of the crowd who, they told us, had a bad back. The men who brought in the sick and lame grabbed four of us from our terrified crowd, and I was one of them. I was lined up behind the man with the bad back. As I looked out to the crowd, gone were the singing, happy faces. Gone were the children who were laughing at my inability to dance. I was going to die.

Chapter 5

Now what? Who am I, really? What is expected of me? What should I do with my life? Do I matter? Please don't be silent, God. I need you.

The witch doctor came back to the forefront of the crowd. Beside him stood the chief of this ultimatum. Would these be the last two faces I ever saw, as they gloated over my death? I looked back to my group, but no one was wanting to replace me at the front line. I saw looks of pity from the faces of those daring to even make eye contact. The fate of four sick people and four tourists were now unceremoniously linked.

My praying comrades and I could do nothing other than lay hands on whom we had been lined up behind. My mind was in shambles. What was I to do? I went to place my hand high up on the back of the man in front of me but had inadvertently placed it on a large round protrusion. I pulled back quickly. Oh no; I was starting to get a feeling and it wasn't good. I put my hand a bit lower down on the other side of his back to get as far away from that last cyst shaped thing as I could but instead found a second one. Double no. That was when I couldn't restrain my tears anymore. I was scared and I knew there was no escaping my fate. I started to trace my finger down his spine so I wouldn't touch anything further and instead confirmed my suspicion that his spine didn't go straight at all. I now knew why he was put up here with the other lame people. He was definitely one of the four sickest people I'd ever met.

I couldn't think. I couldn't pray. I didn't have the words to say and couldn't get my thoughts together. What does a person say in this situation? Is there an actual Scripture I should quote? If there was, I sure didn't know it. In fact, no Scriptures were coming to mind that seemed appropriate enough. My pity party joined my tears. I knew I should be praying, but I couldn't help thinking I was about to lose everything. I had never prayed over anyone for healing before, and this didn't seem like a beginner's introduction. I continued tracing his crooked spine with my finger and tried to gather my wits, but it was all to no avail. The thought, "Through faith are you healed," popped into my head, and I resigned myself to defeat. There's no way I have faith for this. And this old man hasn't even heard why we're here yet or about God, so he definitely doesn't have faith either. We're all going to die. I wasn't sure how long we had to stand up front with our individual lame partners, so I stood frozen to my spot. As I continued to run my fingers down his curved spine, my tears and my pity party flowed unceasingly as well.

"Ai yi yi yi yi!" My bad-back man started whooping and bending and jumping. Did I just hurt him? The interpreter came running over and chatted briefly with him and announced, "He's been healed." The crowd and I gasped together. What? Who? My guy? How? I was front row and I missed it. I know it wasn't because of me; I was crying about myself. I know I didn't have faith; how did that happen? As I watched the crowd pat at the man's back, I was more confused than ever. It was at that moment I felt the Lord ask me, "Kimberley, do you even know how to physically heal a man?"

"No, Lord."

"Do you think I have to be present for this to happen?"

"Yes, Lord."

"Do you think faith is a gift?"

"Yes, Lord, the gift of faith."

"And do you think I'm the one who gives that gift?"

"Yes, Lord, You are the giver of all gifts, including faith."

"So if you don't know how to heal, and you believe Me to be present and to be the giver of faith, then you know I have faith in abundance if it's in Me to give. I know how to heal and I have the faith for it. I just asked you to be present and represent Me, and you did. You already did your part, now let Me do Mine."

It was almost beyond what I could understand but so simple at the same time. The burden had been lifted. Jesus had shown up. I quickly relayed to the other front line prayers what Jesus had told me and why He is here, and that we were just supposed to represent Him. We all laid hands on the paralyzed woman and then gave her a hand to stand. Jesus had healed her. Then we moved our hands over to the blind man. We covered his eye sockets with our hands and gave Jesus complete freedom. We kept peeking until we noticed him looking back at us … with green eyes. I admit I was perplexed. Should we keep praying until the irises turn brown? But then, if Jesus had chosen green, then green it would be, and everyone who saw him from that moment on would know something was different. That was his story to share. With three of the people now fully healed, there was electricity in the air for the ultimate impossible. This boy needed a whole new knee and lower leg. We all placed our hands around the void of air in the shape of a new leg and declared God's love all over these people, and on this boy. We kept praying until we felt something touching our hands. It was beautiful. It was strong. It was perfect. It was a leg and a foot which matched his other foot, but without years of scars and calluses. Jesus, the giver of faith, the Creator of all, had just healed all and saved us in order to help us represent Him and teach these people about faith.

Jesus couldn't be stopped. We awaited the chief's inspection and approval to show the movie. Again the chief spoke to the crowd and we awaited the interpretation. The chief had agreed that all four had been healed. Yes, we could show the movie. We cheered. But the chief was now laying new conditions on those who stayed to watch. Our hearts lurched. What would he choose? What would his conditions be? Would people stay?

The conditions were going to be against anyone who stayed, watched the movie and then decided to forsake their Muslim religion to believe in Christianity. They were required to be exiled from their family, they were required to turn over anything of value to the community leaders, and they were only going to be given one day grace before they were hunted down to be killed. Why would anyone stay with those conditions? What chance do we have now of anyone becoming a believer if tomorrow they die? I thought about altar calls in Canada where the last thing we want to do is to make a new believer uncomfortable in front of others; where we make decisions with eyes closed and heads bowed all around them. I felt cheated. One of the most powerful moments I had ever experienced in my life now seemed all for nothing. Not nothing to the first four people, of course, and not nothing to me, but now the rest of the crowd doesn't have the opportunity to hear about who actually performed those miracles.

However, our leader was not dissuaded. He eagerly cranked up the generator and started the movie. We, as a group, stood on the other side of the truck and were able to watch the reverse image of the movie—a movie about our precious Lord who spoke in a language we didn't know, yet we knew what He had to say throughout the show. We prayed silently and joined hands to show that our hearts were joined as well. I was surprised by how many stuck around to watch. Maybe they thought they could just watch, but were strong enough to stick to their original faith. Maybe they were curious. Maybe standing with an air of disinterest was their mask. We kept praying. As the hours passed, we could see the crowd start to understand and engage with what they were witnessing. Personally, I went from praying they'd stay and listen, to praying with a conflicted heart. I wanted them to understand. I wanted them to make a decision for Christ. I wanted them to know who healed tonight. I wanted more for them. But then I thought about what the chief demanded of them. I didn't want them to lose their families or their possessions. I definitely didn't want them to lose their lives. I couldn't watch them hour after hour without seeing the revelation begin to uncloud their eyes—eyes that would be permanently shut tomorrow when they were killed. Tonight, this crowd could have been responsible for my death if Christ hadn't shown up. Tomorrow I would feel responsible for theirs because He did.

As the movie neared the moment of the Cross, the crowd understood what was imminent. They began to pitch their spears at the Roman soldiers who whipped Christ—spears that pierced the screen only and caused us to spread out from behind the truck. Christ was hung on a cross to die, and when

He did there were those in the crowd who dropped to their knees and cried aloud. But when the stone was rolled away from His grave and Christ appeared to the disciples, that same conquering power of death was also alive in those in front of me right now. Cheers filled the night air. There was no further explanation needed for what they had just witnessed. That was when they crowd rushed upon us.

They turned their attention all at once as if on cue and swarmed around each of us. People started lifting our hands and putting them on their heads. Others beside them would take our hands off of others' heads and put them on their own. This kept happening forcefully and quickly. We asked the interpreter what they were asking us to pray for. Was it for salvation? Did they need a healing? The interpreter's response was we were simply to keep saying, "Be healed in the name of Jesus, Amen." So all I could do was to chant those words as my arms took on a life of their own as they were placed on heads and sores and children.

Acts 2:3 says, "Then, what looked like flames or tongues of fire appeared and settled on each of them." And I was able to witness such an event in my lifetime as well. Those whose hands we touched ignited in flames above their heads. I thought at first it was something I was seeing in the spiritual realm, but as others from my group exclaimed what I was seeing, I realized it was being seen by all who were present. Then the flames spread to those who were far back in the crowd and hadn't reached us at all. The flames spread and when it began to light up the crowd and the night sky, we were able to see the crowd, in fact, hadn't left, but had grown during the movie. There were more people now than I even knew had gathered.

The interpreter sought me out and asked if I would pray for a deaf man. I agreed and was led off to the side. There wasn't just one person; he had lined them up. As I touched their ears, I thought back to earlier. I was just supposed to be present. Christ wants them healed and He will do it. One by one they had started repeating what I had whispered in their ears. There were multiple shouts of, "Amen!" and "Hallelujah!" and "Praise God!" declarations to Heaven. I wished I had known their language so they weren't left with only English words, but I assumed God had a plan for that as well and would rectify it in time.

One sweet mom came with her very young child and the interpreter told me the child might be deaf but was also born paralyzed—it was hard to tell. I could see the flame on the mother. She believed for a miracle, and this time, so did I. This time I knew my faith had grown to where I expected God to show up. My prayers had grown as confident as my faith and the only tears I shed now were ones of excitement and joyous emotions that I couldn't keep bottled up. God was here in our midst and there was nothing He couldn't accomplish. We just had to ask. So with faith and tears for this mother's request, I held the limp child in my arms. Heaven was moved and the child began to twitch. Then with realization in his eyes that someone very foreign looking was holding him, he lifted his arms to his mother for rescue. He was healed.

No matter who they lined up of the sick, the paralyzed, the blind, or the deaf, Christ's power was sufficient for all. The flames over their heads were our signal of their change in beliefs. I don't know where all the people came from or which village they were going to return to, but I did notice that the chief and witch doctor were no longer lingering around. I prayed they were just somewhere in the sea of flames themselves.

We continued long into the night until even the excitement of what was happening before us couldn't stave off our sheer exhaustion. It was time to set up my little red dome and debrief with Christ as I slipped into some much needed sleep.

Chapter 6

Now what? Who am I, really? What is expected of me? What should I do with my life? Do I matter? Please don't be silent, God. I need you.

I awoke with high expectations for the day. We milled around each other's tents while discussions were being held amongst the leaders. It was decided we would do a prayer walk. We were divided into much smaller groups and given one of the pastors in training as our interpreter. We were allowed to walk the desert, see who we come across, and be open to what God wanted us to do. We understood we may come across someone who had been at the service the night before, but we may also come across someone who may be angry about it—so once again we were given the choice to walk or stay with the tents. I chose to walk. I was seeing a pattern of God looking after me if I would just let Him. I was also excited to meet up with people from last night, and to find out their stories.

I remember being invited into some huts and barred from others. I remember invitations from people who were excited both to see us and to introduce their neighbors. I remember one of the first people we came across excitedly grabbed my hand and then we ran—we ran a long ways past many wondering people and children alike to her final destination. Here, there was an old woman laying on a fraying mat barely held together by weathered and dried up leaves. The woman was as weathered as the mat and just as frail. It didn't take long to realize on this mat was where she lived, with small food bowls at the front edge and a sparse blanket over her legs. She was paralyzed. The eager woman who had brought me had a plan, and that plan involved faith; faith was definitely something that was beginning to grow in me. So we prayed, we were present, we represented, and we joined our faith with the faith of Christ and the memories of His power from last evening. And the power of God showed up. I remember the woman yelling out that it felt like her legs were on fire. She was very excited, as she hadn't felt anything in them prior to that.

The previously paralyzed woman who was now dancing and jumping gathered many witnesses. They had all known her, as she was definitely older than the crowd that had gathered. Their questions were being answered by the eager woman who had brought me. I realized this woman had woken up yesterday a Muslim, had done her early morning prayers, and had probably spent most of the day living life on repeat. Last night had changed her. Her faith this morning had changed her even more. And now here we are, less than 12 hours later, and she was preaching to this village about the power of God. One real moment with Christ changes us irrevocably. Even though I don't know what she said, I definitely received my cue when she lined up some of those who stood around and lifted my hand to put on their heads. Again, I prayed my best prayer that they would know the love of the Father in Heaven.

The day was full; we walked many miles and prayed over

the diseased and well alike. Although I didn't understand the language, I understood the heart. It was easy to separate the eager from the distrusting. Even for those ones though, I reached a better understanding of the Father's heart over them, and my love for the nation grew. I was so glad I hadn't let fear win. I was so glad I had gotten on that plane and into that truck and out here into the bush.

We repeated this pattern for three days of walking, of praying, of seeing the miraculous. Part of me wanted this to go on forever, but we were all nearing exhaustion, so it was again with mixed emotions when we heard we were returning to the orphanage. We shared stories amongst ourselves in the back of that truck, and each new story we heard was as exciting as the ones we had witnessed ourselves. We tried to take a tally of how many blind and how many deaf and how many paralyzed were healed, but there were too many to be accurate. That in and of itself was mind-blowing.

The hot wind was blowing us along, but that wasn't what I was feeling. I realized my spirit had been dry and lacking. I wanted more: more of the miraculous, more faith, more of God to quench what I was thirsty for. Thank You, God for challenging me. Growing in faith required me to step out into the unknown. I wanted more unknown. I wanted to live in more opportunities and have God show up in the midst of those moments. I had tasted the miraculous and I was no longer satisfied with the norm.

After a long, bumpy journey home, I was extremely ready for rest. Apparently, one more little detail I had failed to listen to or take information on was that the group was going to a resort to stay for a few days to shower, eat properly, sleep in beds, and pray as a group. I wasn't prepared for a resort, but I also wasn't eager to leave the compound for the luxuries of one. My spirit just couldn't leave this raw experience yet, so I declined to join them. Instead, I was quite happy to set up my little red dome back under the flowering root tree. It didn't take me long to set up as I was getting quite proficient at it by now, and soon I was smoothing the sandy floor for comfort and a good night's sleep.

But a long night's sleep just wasn't what I was going to get. It was still dark when I felt someone shaking me awake. They were trying to pass along news, but I wasn't quite alert enough yet to make sense of the urgency. I followed them out of my tent and to the gate where the truck sat. Others were already there and were passing out the few flashlights the orphanage owned. I took one even though I wasn't sure what we were going to be searching for. I realized it had something to do with me, but I couldn't imagine what I had done that needed a search crew in the middle of the night. I soon found out.

My envelope had gone missing. The envelope I had filled before getting in the truck three days ago had gone missing. The envelope with my money, my identification, my passport, and my return ticket had gone missing. How did that happen? I learned that someone from the group had needed more insulin from their envelope, so they all were handed out at the resort. But I wasn't there. Somehow the decision was made to put my envelope in the truck and let it be driven back to me at the compound, and now it was gone. I panicked. I must have become loud with my thoughts about that decision, as a wise older man came and hugged me. I settled into his chest. I had been warned not to lose those things; that's why they were left behind. I was staying in a compound with no phone, no electricity, no outside contact. I had been told that if something were to happen to my ticket and identification I couldn't get out of the area. Now what?

The truck drove the route to the resort, but neither I nor the passengers in the back with flashlights found the envelope. As we drove away from the resort, making one more pass of the tire marks between, my hope was fading. We closed the compound gates behind the truck and along with it any chance of finding my envelope. I was told to go back to bed and they would look again at first light. I went to bed but sleep didn't join me. I was physically exhausted, but the whirring of my mind and thoughts kept me awake.

Morning came but no good news came with it. They had searched to no avail. They gave me a bottle of water which I could not purchase, and I returned to my little tent to pray. I had no other direction and really didn't know what else to do. I stayed in my tent, I slept some, I prayed some. I remember hearing the kids sing at times. I remember hearing the Muslim prayers being chanted. I remember opening my eyes and it was so dark at times that I could only assume I had gone into another night.

I remember a commotion. I remember very cold water being poured on my face and I remember wondering where they would find cold water in Africa. I hadn't considered that it was me who had heated up past the temperature of lukewarm water. I hadn't considered that actual days had gone by. Many days had gone by. The team had already returned from the resort, and had come to check on me only to find that I had long since run out of water, my one bottle laying empty on my tent floor. I had a fever, making me delirious. I tried to speak, but it all came out incoherently, even to my own ears. I hadn't thought to keep my tent unzipped for air, and I had essentially baked myself in the African heat without water. I know they were giving their best attempt to help me recover, but they fed me trail mix. I also know that sounds like a great idea, but not when that person is allergic to coconut. I am allergic to coconut. So instead of recovering, I went from bad to worse. Now I was really sick.

They tried to explain things to me, but I wasn't fully comprehending. They needed to say good-bye to me; some of them had to leave. I didn't know to where. They were trying to assure me I could stay at the orphanage. I didn't know why. They were handing me the satellite phone again. I was supposed to say good-bye to my family. I tried. I remember being sad that I had missed my daughter's funeral (it was actually my grandmother's funeral, but I was in such a state of delirium, I kept going on about it being my daughter's funeral). I remember telling them I wasn't feeling very good and that I had eaten coconut. I remember them panicking on the phone for details, but I couldn't answer their questions. I remember saying that I was out of water now and had no money to buy more, so I would need them to come as fast as possible because I didn't think I could last long without it. I remember telling them that I would meet them at the tree beside the boy selling trinkets. I remember this good-bye felt final.

By the miraculous provision of Heaven I survived, but I was weak. I was also alone. I knew I had said good-bye to my family who now believed I had perished. Would they still come looking for me even if it was just to collect my remains? My new friends really did have to leave, but the orphanage had warmly opened their arms to me for refuge. There was no extra water or food, but we would pray for provisions together. I tried to help out where I was needed. I slept in my little red tent with my door zippered open and would try to just focus on my new life here, not the one that had slipped away with a lost envelope and sickness. The Scripture that says the joy of the Lord is my strength was transitioning from a bumper sticker nice thing to say into a lifeline of which I had to continually remind myself. I needed that strength to just keep breathing. I needed that joy to not lose faith and hope. The same God who had made the lame to walk, the blind to see, and the deaf to hear was the same God inside the compound as well. He knew of my plight, and He had a plan. I was sure of it. I had to believe that.

But until He revealed that plan, I carried on with the routine of my new life. I sang with the children and taught them English words. I sat with the newly appointed pastors who had come for training. One of them had a Bible with both English and Portuguese, so it helped me find Scriptures for them. I walked to the Indian Ocean and had a daily swim and a large gulp of ocean water to satisfy my thirst for the day.

Chapter 1

Now what? Who am I, really? What is expected of me? What should I do with my life? Do I matter? Please don't be silent, God. I need you.

It was on this beach that I was approached one day by a very angry-looking teenager. I had just come onto the beach from the ocean when he came up very quickly behind me. He glared at me and I froze. He told me that the last white woman he had seen had been in his village years ago. He told me that white woman had come to tell of Christ and his parents became Christians. He told me that he was the one to kill both of them. Now he asked me, "Are you a Christian?"

The question I had forgotten about so many weeks prior was now being asked of me. I knew I could only answer one way, but I also knew what the outcome would be once I stated it. I couldn't help but look around at where I was. It was beautiful. The sun was receding and the sunset was on fire with reds and pinks. I had just swam in the ocean, so I was feeling refreshed. I thought to myself, "What a beautiful place to die." An overwhelming sense of peace washed over me and I knew I felt the presence of the Lord. I assumed He was there to help walk me through this moment and right on to glory. "Yes, I am a Christian." I closed my eyes, and I hoped the blow would be quick. I heard, "There is no condemnation in Christ. There is no condemnation in Christ." I looked to see the boy had fallen to his knees in the sand right before me. He was crying. He told me that everyone else he had asked had said no. He was desperate to find a Christian because he wanted to be prayed for too.

I was overjoyed to pray with this young man. Stephen would go on to become one of my closest friends in Mozambique. We were a great team. He wanted to hear all about the miracles of God, and it was imperative for me to repeat all I had seen and had learned in order to keep reminding myself of the goodness of God. Stephen helped me to never lose sight that God had a good plan for both of us. Stephen knew a bit of English, so it was fun talking to him. He would write words in the sand that he had seen elsewhere, and I would help him read them. I was as poor as he was so he never asked anything of me except to reveal more of God. I was happy to share. Meeting up with Stephen became a joyous event each day, and we would share many laughs.

During one such meeting, as he was writing words in the sand for us to sound out together, he wrote a word that shook my heart. He had just spelled out my surname. "Where did you see that word, Stephen?" He told me a friend of his had a big white envelope and that was the word on the outside of it. I informed him it was my name and inside were my things. I needed that envelope. I had a way home. I told him I didn't care about the money, give it as a reward to whoever found the envelope, but I needed the return paper ticket and my credit card and passport. With hopes as high as ever, we parted with plans to meet the following day and he would bring the envelope with him.

God, You are a genius. Only You could come up with such a remote possibility of a plan to get me home. Only You could put together this friendship and let it be the key I needed to return to my family. I shared with the orphanage staff about my expected package tomorrow. I sang praises the rest of the night to my God. My heart was full of expectancy.

Morning came and the children and I took it as a personal challenge to sing louder than the Muslim prayers. Everything I did that day had a sense of finality to it, that my life was going to change in the afternoon. The joy was palpable. I could hardly await the appointed meeting time, and I set out to be there early.

On my way to the beach I was again appreciating the beautiful scenery that had become my home away from home. I had come to feel a part of the people among whom I walked. I belonged. My desire to be here was being met, although I really longed for my distant home as well. I passed by a police station and decided to stop in. I knew I was early for the beach meeting, so I thought I'd have enough time to notify the local law enforcement that I was going home, therefore I was no longer going to be living at the orphanage down the road. I could now see God's plan of restoration.

I hadn't learned the local language well, and the police chief didn't speak or understand English well, so the conversation on both sides resulted in confusion. That's when the chief asked to come speak with Stephen. At that moment, I thought it was a great plan; they could speak the same language and Stephen could help explain things to him.

But as we walked out of the station and started our journey to the beach, the reality of my error became obvious. The chief told me to point out the thief. I tried to explain that there was no thief. My documents were lost by accident, and there was only a friend who had found them. The chief wouldn't walk beside me. He kept telling me to walk ahead and don't look at him or talk to him. I kept trying to explain that Stephen was my friend; he had done nothing wrong; he was helping me. The chief signaled to his guards and I watched as they fanned out far ahead, encompassing the small beach area. As Stephen came into view waving, the chief wanted to know if that was the thief. He wanted me to point out the thief and then run. I kept trying to tell him there was no thief.

What had I done? In my exuberance for today's meeting, I had forgotten the realities of the land in which I was now living. To steal was an automatic death sentence by the governing militia. Stephen was walking into a trap that I had inadvertently created. I couldn't make the chief understand what I was trying to tell him. Stephen didn't notice the chief at all. What were my options? I could try to walk past Stephen possibly? Make them think I was meeting someone else? I would have to give up on Stephen and my envelope in order to save him. I tried walking away, but Stephen noticed my course correction and changed his own course to intercept. Now what would I do? Stephen and I were going to meet. There was no way to prevent it. Could I explain fast enough that I never called him a thief? Would the chief believe Stephen if he explained my predicament to him? We were too close now for them to suppose I was meeting anyone other than my best friend Stephen. The circle of guards had closed in. They raised their automatic weapons. There was no time for any dialogue or explanation. They opened fire.

What had I done? What had they done? I ran to Stephen's body and tried to cover it with my own. I shouted at them to stop shooting. I shouted that this was my friend. They shouted back to move or get shot too. The sound of bullets was repetitive and deafening. I clenched my eyes and tensed my body awaiting the first of what I assumed would be many pains. We continued to yell back and forth until they expended their cartridges. Then my screaming at them was the only sound on the beach. I was furious. I was traumatized. I was in despair. "Why would you kill him? He did nothing wrong. He was my friend. He was helping me." Some of the guards turned and ran but the chief and a brave few held their ground.

"How did you not get shot?" the chief yelled at me.

"You killed him!" I spat back.

"I'm not dead," Stephen quietly replied from beneath me. I jumped off of Stephen only to see he had his hands on his head, but that he was still very much alive. The chief and I both became simultaneously aware of the circle of bullets and casings around us. He questioned this impossibility while his last brave soldiers also turned and ran. I didn't have any real answers, but in anger and a false sense of bravado, I told him that God didn't want me shot today because I was a Christian. Stephen echoed the same declaration. Now even the chief left.

Stephen and I hugged. We looked at the circle of bullets and the pure, clean sand in the center where we were. God had provided a miracle to defend us—a canopy that stopped the force of every bullet and casing. We were not harmed at all. God had great plans for us, plans to prevent death. He had plans to give us a future, which reminded me that I was going home. "Where is the envelope?" I asked.

"I couldn't find it. I don't have it." He had to be joking, but this really wasn't the moment to joke around.

"Not kidding, where is the envelope?" I asked again, a bit more serious this time. Stephen showed me his empty hands.

He really didn't have it. How could that be? Why would God rescue us but not provide for the envelope? It didn't make sense.

We hugged in our circle. I was elated that we were alive but deflated with no way for me to go home. I was so sure this was the end of my story. I was so sure I had figured out God's genius plan. I said good-bye to Stephen and we made plans to resume our English again tomorrow. Right now I just needed to go be alone. I made my way back to the compound, back past the beautiful surroundings I had admired so lovingly only hours before. I didn't notice them. I had to tell those awaiting my triumphant return that I was empty handed. I crawled into my tent. I wanted to cry, but I knew if I gave in to that, I would allow it to crush my spirit.

God still had a plan; I just didn't know what it was. I had to trust Him in both good times and bad. He protected me today from my own stupidity. He protected Stephen's life from the militia.

I raised up on my knees and decided in my heart that I needed joy to strengthen me, so I chose to sing out my emotions. The words running through my head were *Blessed Be Your Name,* and I sang it at first with what little energy I had left in me. I needed to sing through the feeling of defeat. I needed to praise Him through this circumstance. I needed to recognize that He is in control even when I don't understand.

Blessed be Your name,
when I'm found in the desert place
Though I walk through the wilderness,
Blessed be Your name.
You give and take away,
You give and take away.
My heart will choose to say, Lord blessed be Your name.

The stronger I felt the louder I sang. The louder I sang the stronger I felt. Blessed be Your name.

Blessed be Your name in the land that is plentiful
Where Your streams of abundance flow,
Blessed be Your name.
Every blessing You pour out, I'll turn back to praise.
When the darkness closes in Lord, still I will say,
Blessed be the name of the Lord.

I swung my arms about in my little tent; I sang with all of my heart; I felt refreshed. I needed to see this incident from Heaven's perspective. I needed to feel the power of God renewing my mind. And into that renewed mind I felt the Lord speak to me. He made me realize that I had just lived through what the local tribes had to live through the night the fire fell upon them. I had lost my family. I had lost all of my possessions. I had been found in a life or death situation. And the same God who was caring for His new children out in the desert would also care for me. This trip had helped me release my life to His protection, to His love over me. I had to literally place my life in His hands. But then He asked me, "Would you do it all again knowing what was to come?"

"Yes," I replied. But I also understood that if I knew ahead of time all that was going to happen I would have relied on my own understanding more than His love over me. I could see the increase in my faith life that was grown in adversity. No, I wouldn't change a thing. Help me just to be content in You, Lord, no matter where I live. My life is Yours and I would give up the world to live that life, no matter it's length, under Your direction.

As I swung my arms, I hit someone. I thought I was alone, so it took me by surprise. I looked to see that I had hit a leg—someone had stepped right through the roof of my tent and was now standing in my space. I quickly rolled out of my tent to see who had come and found myself being stared down upon by an enormous angel who looked like a Roman soldier. The children ran up. Some hid behind the tree trunk. Some came to hug me as a protective embrace. I was fixated on the sword and shield he held. Had he come to war against me, or was he already at war to get to me? The angel didn't say anything; it was like he knew my thoughts. He smirked and I figured that was a good sign he wasn't here to war against me. He had something in his hand and he leaned down through my tent top once again and placed something inside.

I couldn't resist. I had to know what it was. I broke eye contact and quickly crawled back inside my dome to see my passport laying on my pillow. I brought it out with thanksgiving in my heart but the angel was gone. I couldn't thank him, but I could thank God for His provision to me. The children and I ran to the orphanage director's office to tell them of what had happened, of the angel, and to show the heavenly provided passport. I imagine we were a commotion, but the directors managed to put together our incoherence into a single train of thought. I believed it meant I was going home now.

I still had no money or other identification, but passports were used for travel, so that is what I felt God was saying. It was time to travel. The supply plane was coming again and although I didn't have a return ticket, I had a testimony and a passport. If that was all God gave me, then I believed it would be enough.

Chapter 8

Now what? Who am I, really? What is expected of me? What should I do with my life? Do I matter? Please don't be silent, God. I need you.

A plan was made. I packed all of my belongings back into my bag and went to meet Stephen on the beach. We had been through so much together, and I longed to take him with me, but I knew I could not. I left him with everything I owned. I told him to sell what he could and keep what he wanted. I showed him the angel-delivered passport and relieved him from his obligation to keep looking for the security envelope. I was going to try to get on the supply plane later today. This was our good-bye. I knew it in my heart.

I also hugged the children and Pastors-in-training one last time before we left the compound for the drive to the landmark tree near where the plane would land. My heart was torn for those left behind. Much like when I had said good-bye to my own family prior, these faces were now family to me. My heart craved to keep them all in my life.

We drove to the plane in silence and only the sound of it landing tore me from my thoughts. We spoke to the pilot, explained my situation, shared my journey with him from plane crash to angel and then showed him my Canadian passport. He agreed to let me fly without a ticket back to his next stop. I would have to figure things out from there, so I agreed.

The pilot landed again without incident. The Lord kept opening doors; I kept retelling my story. I was given passage once again to Johannesburg and was also put on a plane to

Amsterdam. You were doing it, Lord. You were getting me home. I was en-route to Amsterdam, however, when the intercom voice from the pilot started to ebb at my feeling of victory. We were informed that London airport had just been bombed. We were going to be in a short holding pattern once we arrived at Amsterdam, and security was going to be escalated. We were all told to have our documents ready, gather our luggage quickly, and be prepared for long lines through the checkpoints in the airport.

Gathering documents was going to be the easy part—I only had my passport and I had no luggage. The woman at the ticket counter in Johannesburg had put me on the plane without any papers when I had told her I had nowhere else to live and would have to go home with her if she couldn't help me. I didn't even have a boarding pass to show. Of all the days to try to fly around the world without documents and tickets! What is Your plan for this one, Lord? I wondered.

As promised, the lines were long and the security was tight, but the Lord did, indeed, have a plan. It started just as a thought that made me smile, but the Lord increased the joy within me to where I was struggling to keep my giggling to a minimum. This had caught the attention of the security. I was pulled out of line; I laughed outright. I was put in a security room to be searched; I laughed even harder. I knew they were getting angry; I knew they had questions, but I couldn't catch my breath. I kept thinking, "Lord, this is not very helpful. I need their favor right now, not this." Another officer entered the security room and my hysterics increased without my willing it to do so. He was mad from the start. I'm sure they were already having a trying enough day without my crazy involvement. He demanded to know what was so funny, so I shared with him the tiny little thought that initially had made me smile. "The last time I flew into Amsterdam my plane crashed, and now here I am again asking for you to put me on another plane." I did honestly see the humor in it, but it should have remained as a thought in my mind, not something to make me double over in laughter. I also could see why the man stormed out.

I was alone for quite a while before someone else came to visit. Thankfully, by then the Lord had ceased His gift of laughter—a gift I'm not really sure was a gift. But this new man rolled in with him a tall square cart and on top of this cart was an open laptop. He rolled it right up to me to show me what he had been watching. There, on the screen, were all the passengers from the flight that had crashed, as we were walking into the terminal, showing our passports and signing documents to say if we had any injuries or had escaped them. It was me. I was wearing the same clothes I had on right at this moment, carrying the same passport that they had just taken away from me.

He asked for a story, so I gave him one. I explained how after that crash I had kept flying all the way to Mozambique, and I related to him all of the experiences I had and how I had lost everything, but how God had miraculously taken care of me. I apologized for the last gift of God. I really couldn't control it. But now, it was his turn to smile at me in my somber mood. He believed me and was going to return me to where I had flown into Amsterdam that first time.

I slept on the plane, ate free food, and drank as many bottles of water as they would give me. I landed without incident back into the United States. From there, and with one more retelling of my testimony, it was declared I would be Canada's problem. I was happy to oblige and boarded my last plane. I had now flown on five airplanes, through many continents and countries, without purchasing a single ticket, but simply with the power of a testimony.

I returned home to a family I had already said good-bye to. The greatest desire my heart had ever experienced had been fulfilled. I was brought through the highs and lows of life and trauma and came out the other side with an overabundance of faith in the goodness of God. No, I wouldn't change a thing. One day I am going to be invited to sit around a dining room table and tell stories of my missionary experiences to unbelievers. These stories may sound a bit scary at first, maybe even like a rollercoaster, but I promise to explain where the grace and mercy of my Lord comes in.

I have seen too much to forget it. I have learned too much to walk away. I am changed and it was all due to a still small voice that whispered in my ear when I sat still at His feet and asked what the God of the Universe wanted to do with my simple little life.

I am forever changed by a whisper.

CPSIA information can be obtained
at www.ICGtesting.com
Printed in the USA
LVHW081424140622
721248LV00010B/320